W9-BEB-488

# Speaking
## of
# Graduating...

# Speaking
## of
# Graduating...

Excerpts from Timeless
Graduation Speeches

*compiled and edited*

by

**Alan Ross**

WG
WALNUT GROVE PRESS
NASHVILLE, TENNESSEE

©2001 Walnut Grove Press

All rights reserved. Except for brief quotes used in reviews, articles, or other media, no part of this book may be reproduced or transmitted in any form or by any means, electronic or mechanical, including photocopying, recording, or by information storage or retrieval system, without permission by the publisher.

WALNUT GROVE PRESS
Nashville, TN 37211

ISBN: 1-58334-097-1

*The ideas expressed in this book are not, in all cases, exact quotations, as some have been edited for clarity and brevity. In all cases, the author has attempted to maintain the speaker's original intent. In some cases, material for this book was obtained mostly from secondary sources, primarily print media. While every effort was made to ensure the accuracy of these sources, the accuracy cannot be guaranteed. For additions, deletions, corrections or clarifications in future editions of this text, please write WALNUT GROVE PRESS.*

Printed in the United States of America
Cover Design & Page Layout: *Bart Dawson*
Typesetting & Page Layout: *karol cooper*

1 2 3 4 5 6 7 8 9 10 • 00 01 02 03 04 05 06 07 08 09 10

*for karol*
thank you
for your most beautiful
contribution
to my life

Through our great good fortune,
in our youth
our hearts were touched with fire.

*Pat Collins*
*television personality*
*Simmons College, 1980*

# Table of Contents

# Introduction

The commencement address:

Where else exists a platform that encourages the speaker to wax profoundly philosophical, replete with advice-giving, blue-sky optimism, and shameless attempts at humor?

As with any main event, action circulates on the periphery as well, proving that life inexorably goes on — even though a president may be speaking. In 1999, at Princeton's commencement, salutatorian Thomas Wickham Schmidt ended his speech, delivered entirely in Latin, with a marriage proposal — in English (the intended said yes).

And illustrating that not all commencements should be taken with the seriousness of a final exam, Kermit the Frog, previously no stranger to the likes of both Harvard and Oxford, leaped into scholastic history by accepting an honorary Doctorate of Amphibious Letters while addressing the graduating class at Long Island University's Southhampton College in 1996.

Who says it isn't easy being green?

a.r.

I am not addressing you because you are not letters. Even if you were put in a large package and could be sent bulk mail, I would have nowhere to send you. I am not commencing anything, I did that when I began to talk. You are not commencing anything, at least in the aggregate; I am aware that individuals are always commencing something: some of you are commencing respiration, commencing efforts to stifle yawns, commencing to feel the need for a drink. But as a group, you're just sitting there, and you commenced that already....

*Stephen King*
*author*
*University of Maine, 1988*

# Chapter 1

# Mortarboard
# and Tassel

We endow our commencement speakers with the capacity to explain our times. They become emissaries, visiting representatives of the world that graduates are about to enter.

*Peter J. Smith*
*author, Onward!*

Congratulations! Today is your day. You're off to Great Places! You're off and away. You have brains in your head. You have feet in your shoes. You can steer yourself. Any direction you choose.

*Dr. Seuss*
*author, Oh, the Places You'll Go*
*from the speech by Dr. Rita Colwell*
*University of Connecticut, 2000*

Graduation is where a commencement speaker tells rows and rows of graduates, all dressed exactly the same, that individuality is what makes the world tick.

*Orrin Hatch*
*U.S. Senator, Utah*
*Dixie College*

Graduation day — the high point of college. The commencement speech — the low point of graduation day.

*Robert Novack*
*assoc. prof. of business logistics, Penn State*
*Univ. of Illinois at Champaign-Urbana*

Your families are extremely proud of you. You can't imagine the sense of relief they are experiencing. This would be a most opportune time to ask for money.

*Gary Bolding*
*chairman, Stetson Univ. art department,*
*Stetson University, 1998*

You are in charge of yourselves: that is the underlying principle of the education you have received. You commence this day in the name of civilization.

*E. L. Doctorow*
*writer*
*Sarah Lawrence College, 1983*

Here are some things you can do right after graduation: throw a baseball to a little girl; ask your teacher for his or her autograph; ask your mother or father to dance; throw a kiss to a little old lady; and take a walk in the woods with someone you love.

*Art Buchwald*
*columnist/satirist*
*Vassar College*

I get the feeling that people all over the country are graduating and they're leaving one phase and moving on to another with a combined feeling of anxiety and elation.

*James Taylor*
*singer/songwriter*
*Berklee, 1995*

What everybody — parents and graduates — wants out of the commencement speaker is brevity, wit , then a swift cut to the chase, amen, goodbye.

*Peter J. Smith*

The commencement speech differs from any other type of speech: part memoir, part summation of the year that's already gone by, part tribute to the person the speaker was at age twenty-two, part entertainment and part sermonette. The best of them bring out the best in everyone. They instruct. They warn. They reflect. They advise. They exhort. They persuade. They reassure. And they inspire. Few other kinds of speech possess their peculiar authenticity.

*Peter J. Smith*

Commencement speeches were invented largely in the belief that outgoing college students should never be released into the world until they have been properly sedated.

*Garry Trudeau*
*cartoonist*

There is a good reason they call these ceremonies "commencement exercises." Graduation is not the end; it's the beginning.

*Orrin Hatch*
*Dixie College*

College seniors feel self-conscious in their mortarboard with the tassel, their warlock robes. Their parents and grandparents are crowded behind them in the audience, a blur of faces, hats, purses, and breath mints.

*Peter J. Smith*

You have partaken of the treasure-house of knowledge, one which has been replenished by generations of scholars, researchers, and practitioners.

*Mikhail Gorbachev*
*former USSR president*
*Emory University, 1992*

I left Harvard in 1969 disillusioned by what I saw happening in our country and certain of only one thing about my future: I would never, ever go into politics.

*Al Gore*
*Harvard University, 1994*

Whatever direction you choose to embark on, remember that you have had an opportunity that most people in the world will never have. That is the benefit of a higher education.

*Ahmet Ertegun*
*Atlantic Records*
*Berklee, 1991*

Remember that not getting what you want is sometimes a wonderful stroke of luck. The goal is to view every doorway, even one with a shadow, as an opening to new horizons.

*Dalai Lama's Instructions for Life*
*from Dr. Rita Colwell's commencement speech,*
*University of Connecticut, 2000*

# Chapter 2

# The Big Picture

Life is a journey... every experience is here
to teach you more fully how to be who you
really are.

*Oprah Winfrey*
*TV talk show hostess/actress*
*Wellesley College, 1997*

The victory is not always to the swift,
but to him who finishes the race.

*Orrin Hatch*
*Dixie College*

We must be grateful. Of all the creatures on
this planet, only we have been given this subtle
and marvelous gift of the word. When we are
grateful, we will be happy....

*Mark O'Brien*
*poet/journalist/inspirational voice for the disabled*
*Berkeley, 1997*

Education does not develop your character
until it merges with integrity and wisdom.

*Sam Nunn*
*U.S. Senator, Georgia*
*Emory University, 1981*

God speaks in the silence of the heart.
Listening is the beginning of prayer.

*Mother Teresa*
*humanitarian*
*Georgetown University, 1982*

Every generation has the obligation to free
men's minds for a look at new worlds, to look
out from a higher plateau than the last
generation.

*James Lovell*
*astronaut*
*Western Montana College, 1983*

We are more alike than different from one another. We — your parents, your grandparents, and I — are simply at different stages along the same journey as you. Study us well. And if you look very closely, you will also find yourselves twenty or thirty or forty years from now. But take pride in the fact that, for all the universality, each of you carries within him or her a spark of uniqueness.

*Ted Koppel*
*broadcaster*
*Syracuse University, 1982*

People who have studied happiness have found that a satisfying job is important for happiness, but not as important as a good marriage or a good relationship with friends.

*Wyndham Robertson*
*former assistant managing editor,* Fortune
*Hollins College, 1983*

The gentle revolution...is the revolt against violence and against impersonal power.... The gentle revolution springs from the imperative need to bring imagination, tenderness, human compassion to bear in regions where they have often been denied access.... The people engaged in this revolution will not be asking where the jobs are; they will be asking where the need is.

*May Sarton*
*writer*
*Clark University*

Despite wise preparation and hard work, life sometimes takes some detours when you cannot make things happen exactly as you envisioned. It may sound Pollyanna-like to suggest that what feels like a disappointment is very often an opportunity in disguise, but I'll say it anyway.

*Dr. Rita Colwell*
*National Science Foundation*
*University of Connecticut, 2000*

You should be warned that it becomes increasingly easy, as you get older, to drown in nostalgia. In fact, you can almost measure where you are in life by the degree to which you have begun looking back, rather than ahead. Time doesn't pass — we do, hurtling across the face of a continuum. A snap of the finger is the passing of a generation.

*Ted Koppel*
*Syracuse University, 1982*

I am convinced that it is not the fear of death that haunts our sleep so much as the fear that our lives will not have mattered.

*Rabbi Harold Kushner*
*from a speech by Sue Suter*
*Robert Morris College, 1996*

Success and its hand-in-glove partner, failure, are equally difficult to handle, and everyone has to deal with both in different quantities in their lifetimes.

*George Martin*
*Beatles producer*
*Berklee, 1989*

We must lead humanity's everlasting effort to live harmoniously with nature, employing the technology through the enrichment of spirit as well as body, and we will.

*Gerald Ford*
*38th president of the United States*
*University of Pennsylvania, 1975*

Nothing important, or meaningful, or beautiful, or interesting, or great ever came out of imitations. The thing that is really hard is giving up on being perfect and beginning the work of becoming yourself.

*Anna Quindlen*
*writer*
*Mount Holyoke College, 1999*

The uniqueness of human life is that it has done, and can do, the impossible.

*Norman Cousins*
*writer*
*Lawrence University, 1975*

Almost everything is more complicated than it seems, but almost nothing is hopeless.

*Vincent Barnett*
*former president, Colgate University*
*Williams College, 1975*

You count. You make a difference. You can add to the sum of beauty and joy and love and understanding in the world, or you can subtract from those already scarce commodities. *What you do matters.*

*Vincent Barnett*
*Williams College, 1975*

In a higher world it is otherwise, but here below to live is to change, and to be perfect is to have changed often.

*Martin Marty*
*professor*
*Lawrence University, 1976*

There is so much still to be done. You still can choose to be a pioneer.

*Stephen Breyer*
*U.S. Supreme Court Justice*
*Stanford, 1997*

If you do feel a little worried, don't worry about being worried.

*Tracy Kidder*
*writer*
*Sarah Lawrence College, 1986*

Think for yourselves. Let me repeat it: just think for yourselves.

*Lee Iacocca*
*former head of Chrysler Corporation*
*Duke University, 1986*

We've developed an enormous cultural passivity. We spend so much of our time and attention as spectators, viewers, listeners, part of a vast, faceless audience. That makes for a synthetic kind of existence. Without personal participation, a sense of reality fades away, and then it becomes hard to identify values, set priorities, to think and feel with any depth.

*Flora Lewis*
*writer*
*Clark University, 1986*

Believe in something larger than yourself. Get involved in some of the big ideas of our time.

*Barbara Bush*
*wife of the 41st president of the United States*
*Wellesley College, 1989*

You cannot fully understand your own life without knowing and thinking beyond your life, your own neighborhood, and even your own nation.

*Johnnetta Cole*
*anthropologist*
*Grinnell College, 1990*

The best thing you can give yourselves for graduation is the gift of possibility. And the best thing you can give each other is the pledge to go on protecting that gift in each other as long as you live.

*Paul Newman*
*actor*
*Sarah Lawrence College, 1989*

We cannot live for ourselves alone. Our lives are connected by a thousand invisible threads, and our actions run as causes and return to us as results.

*Herman Melville*
*from the speech by Vernon Jordan*
*DePauw University, 1993*

I think that it is important to look at the long view as you go out of here and realize that there's a long time ahead, and there is time to see it all, to do it all, and to do it in ways that make you proud and happy in the end.

*Cokie Roberts*
*TV journalist*
*Wellesley College, 1994*

The last frontier today, other than the distant reaches of the stars, is the human brain. It is our brains, not our brawn, that will move us forward.

*Jane Alexander*
*actress*
*Smith College, 1999*

Material possessions rust away, wear away, or
depreciate. Character alone will never tarnish.

*Elizabeth Dole*
*wife of former Sen. Robert Dole*
*Dartmouth College, 1991*

Turn your wounds into wisdom.

*Oprah Winfrey*
*Wellesley College, 1997*

Ladies and Gentlemen:
Start you engines.

*James Olson*
*vice president of the board, AT&T*
*DePauw University, 1981*

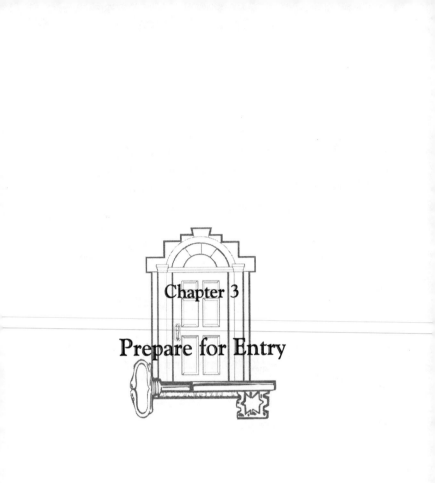

# Chapter 3

# Prepare for Entry

You have an interesting journey ahead — one that will take you in directions you can't possibly predict and draw on knowledge you don't even know you possess.

*Raymond W. Smith*
*chairman/CEO, Bell Atlantic*
*Carnegie Mellon University, 1997*

You must never stop learning. Read. Enjoy music and art. Visit new places. Try food from a foreign country. Find some new constellations in the night sky. Keep your mind working and your outlook fresh.

*Orrin Hatch*
*Dixie College*

I know what you are thinking: you don't know what you want to do. Well, who ever did at your age? Take a few years to find out what you want to do. Take as many as five.

*Wyndham Robertson*
*Hollins College, 1983*

Every new change will also bring new
opportunities — unimagined
opportunities — for those
who are ready.

*Bill Frist*
*U.S. Senator, Tennessee*
*East Tennessee State University*

Character education is a life-long process that begins at home, continues through the spirit and atmosphere of our schools, and into our work places. You must take this to heart, and "Try not to become a person of success," as Einstein said, "but rather try to become a person of value."

*General Henry H. Shelton*
*chairman, Joint Chiefs of Staff*
*North Carolina State University, 1998*

Mistakes, no matter how bad they seem, are survivable; we can even grow from them.

*Sue Suter*
*former U.S. Commissioner of Rehabilitation*
*Robert Morris College, 1996*

Every time you make a step toward your goal — by practicing, performing, and finally accomplishing one thing that you wanted to accomplish — you build on your success.

*Chick Corea*
*musician*
*Berklee, 1997*

When you are deciding what to do, don't do it because it's safe and sensible or because others expect it. Do something because you love it so much you'll be miserable if you don't.

> *Denise Di Novi*
> *film producer*
> *Simmons College, 1997*

Because then, work is no longer work. It is what you enjoy doing the most. Your goal does not have to be grand or grandiose. But it has to be something that you dedicate yourself to.

> *Ahmet Ertegun*
> *Berklee, 1991*

Everyone has opportunities of one sort or another throughout their lives, and one cannot expect to benefit from every one. The trick is to recognize the break when it comes and to take advantage of it.

> *George Martin*
> *Berklee, 1989*

A self that has been nurtured will lead you to what you really want to do. There is no one plan that is workable. There isn't one way of doing it that is best. But there is something to be said for passion. There's something to be said for caring deeply.

*Wendy Wasserstein*
*playwright*
*Mount Holyoke College, 1990*

Do not turn your head away from injustice. Do not stop believing you can make a difference.

*Anthony Lewis*
*journalist*
*Williams College, 1978*

A knowing mind will ultimately win out, if anything can, against a loud voice.

*Juanita Kreps*
*U.S. Secretary of Commerce*
*Duke University, 1977*

Studies have proven that students returning home after four years away at college tend to get agoraphobia when having to sleep in a room with less than fourteen people in it. If it's difficult at first, sleep in a WMCA dormitory for a few days, then try a small hospital ward with four to six people until you're ready to come back to a room of your own.

*Neil Simon*
*playwright*
*Williams College, 1984*

We sense that you are all much brighter than we are. You speak a language that is almost foreign to us. You can read digital printouts. You know what astuteness reading is. And what is particularly disturbing is that you all come out at the same time — June — in hordes with your dark graduation cloaks darkening the earth. Why is it, I ask, that you can't be squeezed out one at a time like peach pits?

*George Plimpton*
*writer*
*Hobart and William Smith Colleges, 1978*

You want work that is rewarding and altruistic, that is worth doing for its own sake, not just for the price it commands. Those opportunities can appear in unexpected places, and some of them, maybe the best of them, you have to invent.

*Tracy Kidder*
*Sarah Lawrence College, 1986*

One early mistake that most of us tend to make is to expect that our careers will take a linear, upward course. That expectation can lead to discouragement.

*Sue Suter*
*Robert Morris College, 1996*

When luck goes against you, don't let it get you down; it will all even out in the end.

*George Martin*
*Berklee, 1989*

I wish you much joyful weirdness
in your lives.

*Gary Larson*
*cartoonist*
*Washington State University, 1990*

You have to do what you enjoy. Anything else is a waste of time.

> *Malcolm Forbes*
> *industrialist*
> *Syracuse University, 1988*

There is no free lunch. Don't feel entitled to anything you don't sweat and struggle for.

> *Marian Wright Edelman*
> *founder/director, Children's Defense Fund*
> *University of Illinois at Champaign-Urbana, 1993*

I refuse to offer homilies in spite of an almost insurmountable urge to talk about what will happen as you row the canoe of your life down the river of the future, except to say that you will undoubtedly encounter the sandbars of confusion and the rapids of adversity.

*Stephen King*
*University of Maine, 1988*

When you return home to what you might call "civilian life" after four years away, there will be a certain period of adjustment. You don't have to drop completely the casual style of attire you've been used to, but you may want to start wearing shoes on the right foot as well as the left.

*Neil Simon*
*Williams College, 1984*

A substantial part of what lies ahead of you is going to be claimed by boredom.

*Joseph Brodsky*
*poet*
*Dartmouth College, 1989*

Your degree does not automatically qualify you for a successful career or even for an immediate job. You will still have to fight to make your way, and you will be better equipped due to your work and achievement during your education.

*Ahmet Ertegun*
*Berklee, 1991*

Love your work. If you always put your heart into everything you do, you really can't lose. Whether you wind up making a lot of money or not, you will have had a wonderful time, and no one will ever be able to take that away from you.

*Alan Alda*
*actor*
*Connecticut College, 1980*

Through discipline and organization and preparation, and especially inspiration, you finally end up with the capacity to do something that you didn't know you could do.

*Pat Matheney*
*musician*
*Berklee, 1996*

Survival tip number one for going into the real world is to bring a map with you — a map, by the way, of yourself. Don't listen to others for directions about who you are.

*Diane Sawyer*
*University of Illinois at Champaign-Urbana, 1997*

Read, read, read, is my commencement advice.
*David McCullough*
*University of Connecticut, 1999*

Recall the wisdom of Walker Percy, who wrote, "Do not be the kind of person who gets all A's but flunks ordinary living."

*Mark Shield*
*political commentor*
*University of Notre Dame, 1997*

It is important to have determination and optimism and patience. If you lack patience, even when you face some small obstacle, you lose courage. There is a Tibetan saying, "Even if you have failed at something nine times, you must continue and not lose hope." I think that is important. Use your brain to analyze the situation. Do not rush through it, but think. Once you decide what to do about that obstacle, then there is a possibility to achieve your goal.

*The Dalai Lama*
*spiritual leader*
*Emory University, 1998*

Above all else: go out with a sense of humor. It is needed armor. Joy in one's heart and some laughter on one's lips is a sign that the person down deep has a pretty good grasp of life.

*Hugh Sidey*
*writer*
*Coe College, 1995*

At commencement you wear your
square-shaped mortarboards. My hope is
that from time to time you will
let your minds be bold,
and wear sombreros.

*Paul Freund*
*professor*
*Clark University, 1977*

Chapter 4

One Can
Only Hope

We live by hope. We do not always get all we want when we want it. But we have to believe that someday, somehow, some way, it will be better, and that we can make it so.

*Hubert Humphrey*
*former U.S. Vice President*
*University of Pennsylvania, 1977*

Our faith can guide our vision. It can direct our actions. It can be a strong foundation for our careers, our communities, our families, our government, and our own happiness.

*Orrin Hatch*
*Dixie College*

Intelligence fueled by hope and faith and courage is what will save us. A willingness to believe in something beyond ourselves. And yes, I do mean some infinite power that infuses our existence with a meaning that transcends the simple span of our lives.

*Ted Koppel*
*Tufts University, 1994*

Culture is not enough; there must be an ethical dimension to whatever you study. It is up to you to change, to disarm evil. In spite of what I lived through, I do have faith, and in spite of the fact that I know I cannot talk, I must talk; I must share. I must tell you how great, how compassionate, how just the human being must be. It is our only hope.

*Elie Wiesel*
*writer*
*Hobart and Smith College, 1982*

I hope that you have someone you can look up to, whether it is a brother, a friend, a parent, or just an acquaintance. Having role models is an important part of knowing who you are and, more importantly, who you want to become.

*Ahmet Ertegun*
*Berklee, 1991*

The optimist believes in the triumph of hope over expectations. My favorite definition of which is: An accordion player with a beeper.

*Ted Koppel*
*Tufts University, 1994*

Peace need not be impracticable, and war need not be inevitable. By defining our goal more clearly, by making it seem more manageable and less remote, we can help all peoples to see the goal of peace, to draw hope from it, and to move irresistibly toward it.

*John F. Kennedy*
*35th president of the United States*
*Yale, 1963*

If money is your only pursuit, you may wake up one day to find that you've thrown away a very interesting life: yours.

*Tracy Kidder*
*Sarah Lawrence College, 1986*

Dare to believe that the future can be better than the past. Dare to believe that among our midst there have been optimists who have planted seeds, so that you can reap the harvest. And then, encouraged by their example, do the same for your children. Life is not easy, but you must dare to hope.

*Ted Koppel*
*Tufts University, 1994*

We might as well dream of the
world as it ought to be.

*Toni Morrison*
*writer*
*Sarah Lawrence College, 1988*

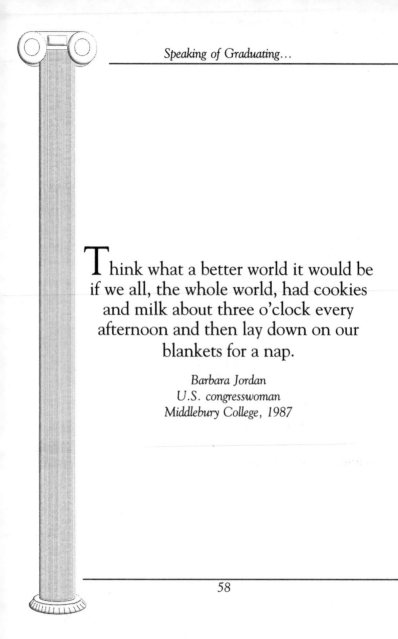

Think what a better world it would be if we all, the whole world, had cookies and milk about three o'clock every afternoon and then lay down on our blankets for a nap.

*Barbara Jordan*
*U.S. congresswoman*
*Middlebury College, 1987*

If you have not yet developed any prayers of your own, now is the time to start. There is no question in my own mind that failure is the foundation on which the greatest prayers are built, and that one can never fully savor the satisfactions of accomplishment unless one can contrast the feelings of hopes dashed or goals missed.

*James B. Stewart*
*writer*
*DePauw University, 1989*

I'm a prisoner of hope, even when there's evidence to the contrary. William James said it so well when he talked about faith being the courage to act when doubt is warranted.

*Cornel West*
*professor/writer*
*Wesleyan University, 1993*

It's better to be a hopeful person than a cynical, grumpy one, because you have to live in the same world either way, and if you're hopeful, you have more fun.

*Barbara Kingsolver*
*writer*
*DePauw University, 1994*

Life really must have joy.
It's supposed to be fun!

*Barbara Bush*
*Wellesley College, 1989*

The first lesson I often offer is that life is full of second chances.

*Steve Kroft*
*broadcaster*
*Syracuse University, 1996*

If we are to evolve and become truly great, there must be an amphitheater big enough to hold everyone — young, old, rich, poor, black, white, yellow, blue, brindle, laughing, crying, and feeling safe together.

*Zoe Caldwell*
*actress*
*Barnard College, 1999*

Create the highest, grandest vision possible for your life, because you become what you believe.
*Oprah Winfrey*
*Wellesley College, 1997*

This is the hard work of your life in the world: to make it all up as you go along, to acknowledge the introvert, the clown, the artist, the reserved, the distraught, the goofball, the thinker.

*Anna Quindlen*
*Mount Holyoke College, 1999*

# Chapter 5

# The Human Condition

Our greatest living philosopher — Snoopy, in the cartoon strip *Peanuts* — says that no problem is so big or so complicated that it cannot be run away from. But I urge you not to run away from problems. Keep alive the spirit of inquiry which, with any luck, you have learned here. Keep your circle of acquaintances wide, so that you will always have fresh points of view. I hope that you will listen to your critics. If you can't answer them adequately, maybe they have something. And finally, I pray that you will worry if you start sounding like everyone else you know.

*Jane Bryant Quinn*
*writer*
*Middlebury College, 1981*

Knowledge is what happens when you're not looking.

*Raymond W. Smith*
*Carnegie Mellon University, 1997*

Whenever I feel confused, stressed or unhappy, or am in crisis, I go to school.

> Mark O'Brien
> Berkeley, 1997

It was through my series of mistakes that I learned I could be a better Oprah.

> Oprah Winfrey
> Wellesley College, 1997

I suppose I became successful by a combination of dumb luck, low cunning, and risk-taking born out of curiosity.

> Sting
> singer/composer
> Berklee, 1994

Freedom of conscience, respect for each individual, tolerance, sympathy, the ability to put oneself in another's place: These are the qualities we need as we enter the new era.

> Mikhail Gorbachev
> Emory University, 1992

The day you stop learning is the day you begin decaying…

*Isaac Asimov*
*writer*
*Connecticut College, 1975*

As human beings, we need to know that we are not alone, that we are not crazy or that we are all completely out of our minds, that there are other people out there who feel as we do, who live as we do, who love as we do, who are like us.

*Billy Joel*
*musician*
*Berklee, 1993*

There's always the knowledge that the work itself is the reward, and if I choose challenging work, it'll pay me back with interest.

*Meryl Streep*
*actress*
*Vassar College, 1983*

When faced with the inevitable, you always have a choice. You may not be able to alter reality, but you can alter your attitude toward it.

*Margaret Atwood*
*University of Toronto, 1983*

The ancients said: primum vivere, deinde philosophari — meaning, first live and then philosophize. The coming era will prompt us to turn this maxim upside down and state: First philosophize!

*Mikhail Gorbachev*
*Emory University, 1992*

Cynicism is deadly. It bites everything it can reach — like a dog with a foot caught in a trap. And then it devours itself. It drains us of the will to improve; it diminishes our public spirit; it saps our inventiveness; it withers our souls.

*Al Gore*
*Harvard University, 1994*

As a culture we seem to feel uneasy and
skeptical about anything that doesn't have a
number attached to it that represents money in
the bank.

*James Taylor*
*singer/songwriter*
*Berklee, 1995*

We live surrounded by records, if anything
overwhelmed with documentary evidence,
bombarded by more information about history
— and about everything else — than we can
possibly assimilate. In some ways life today is
like life in a museum.

*Christopher Lasch*
*sociologist*
*Middlebury College, 1981*

Keep your old love letters. Throw away your
old bank statements.

*Mary Schmich*
*journalist*
*Chicago Tribune, 1997*

If your success is not on your own terms, if it looks good to the world but does not feel good in your heart, it is not really success in the truest sense.

*Anna Quindlen*
*Mount Holyoke College, 1999*

Everyone is allowed a little failure now and again. The reassuring thing I have learned from working with geniuses is that no one is perfect; no one is so good that he does not need help.

*George Martin*
*Berklee, 1989*

A little less hypocrisy and a little more tolerance toward oneself can only have good results in respect for our neighbors, for we are all too prone to transfer to our fellows the negative feelings we inflict upon our own natures.

*Carl Jung*
*from the speech by Anna Quindlen,*
*Mount Holyoke College, 1999*

If you don't have a philosophy of life, let me
warn you that the world you are about to enter
is a dangerous place to go looking for one.

*James Gannon*
*editor,* Des Moines Register
*Coe College, 1988*

There is always the risk that advice reflects the
tunnel vision of one's own career. Supposedly
someone asked Conrad Hilton what he might
pass on to others after 50 years in the hotel
business and he replied, "Always keep the
shower curtain inside the bathtub."

*Stephen Breyer*
*Stanford, 1997*

Imitations are redundant.
Your self is what is wanted.

*Anna Quindlen*
*Mount Holyoke College*
*May 23, 1999*

Our society needs the essential quality of enthusiasm, the interest which fires people and makes it unnecessary for them to ask, "What is the point of my life?" Some people have enthusiasm in abundance. Be sure you're one of those people.

*Flora Lewis*
*Clark University, 1986*

To accomplish great things,
we must dream as well as act.

*Anatole France*
*from the speech by businessman Leonard Lauder*
*Connecticut College, 1989*

Stop trying to be different. You don't
have to be different to be good. To be
good is different enough.

*Arthur Freed*
*from a speech by the Red Cross'*
*Bernadine Healy*
*Ohio State University, 1992*

One of the things you have to face is the unpleasant fact that you will not ever arrive at any condition of life with which you are totally, permanently satisfied. It seems unfortunate, but it's true, that to experience real happiness, you first, or occasionally anyway, have to be unhappy. So you're going to be unhappy sometimes. Just accept it as part of the process.

*Andy Rooney*
*TV commentator, addressing his alma mater*
*Colgate University, 1996*

Optimism is the quality that allows us to triumph over despair. It requires courage and a willingness to dare.

*Ted Koppel*
*Tufts University, 1994*

Humor makes us free. That may seem like an odd conclusion, but as long as the tyrant cannot control the minds of free men, they remain free. Humor abounded behind the Iron Curtain and in POW camps. Humor also is our way of dealing with the inexplicable.

*Bob Newhart*
*comedian*
*Catholic University, 1997*

There will be times when crisis is going to feel overwhelming. But whenever it starts to get you down, just remember one thing. Remember that the Chinese word for "crisis" is composed of two picture characters — one for the word "danger" and one for the word "opportunity."

*Norman B. Rice*
*professor*
*Whitman College, 1998*

All creative people are dissatisfied with themselves at one time or another. That too is part of the process. Then after indulging in glorious self-pity, they get back at it again. And again. And they work, and they suffer, and they understand, at the bottom, that there is nothing, absolutely nothing, that's as much fun as this.

*Jules Feiffer*
*cartoonist/satirist*
*Southhampton College, 1999*

Education and the warm heart, the compassionate heart — if you combine these two, then your education, your knowledge, will be constructive. Then you yourself become a happy person.

*The Dalai Lama*
*Emory University, 1998*

 Talent is possibility; ability is the knack of getting a certain thing right more often than you get it wrong; creativity is a mixture of both.

*Stephen King*
*University of Maine, 1988*

Don't spend a lot of time worrying about your failures. I've learned a whole lot more from my mistakes than from all of my successes.

*Ann Richards*
*former governor of Texas*
*Mount Holyoke College, 1995*

It is not a sprint that you
are running;
it is more like a marathon.
And remember,
you have to keep running.

*George Martin*
*Berklee, 1989*

Chapter 6

Taking the Challenge

Begin challenging your own assumptions.
Your assumptions are your windows on the
world. Scrub them off every once in awhile,
or the light won't come in.

*Alan Alda*
*Connecticut College, 1980*

Diversity — like anything worth having —
requires effort. Effort to learn about and respect
differences, to be compassionate with one
another, to cherish our own identity ... and to
accept unconditionally the same in others.

*Barbara Bush*
*Wellesley College*

Be prepared to adapt.
Be willing to risk.
Be eager to dream.

*Bill Frist*
*East Tennessee State University*

Each one of us has special talents and abilities to add to the tapestry we call community. Never, ever accept the limits of labels that would rob the world of your abilities.

*Sue Suter*
*Robert Morris College, 1996*

Don't be afraid of trying, of dreaming. Don't even be afraid of failure or tears. We all stumble. We all face fear, and that's what makes us human.

*George Bush*
*41st president of the United States*
*The Johns Hopkins University, 1996*

$A$re people capable of rising above their private, group, and local interests? Today, the fate of humanity depends on it.

*Mikhail Gorbachov*
*Emory University, 1992*

$H$ere comes my piece of advice: be certain that what you're doing is not merely a job, but that your work is the thing that you really want to do.

*Frances Fitzgerald*
*writer*
*Sarah Lawrence College, 1982*

$L$ike every past generation, we must move on from the reassuring repetition of stale phrases to a new, difficult, but essential confrontation with reality.

*John F. Kennedy*
*Yale, 1963*

No exercise is better for the human heart than reaching down and lifting someone else up, to serve others, and to enrich your community. This truly defines a successful life. For success is personal, and it is charitable, and it is the sum, not of our possessions, but of how we help others.

*George Bush*
*The Johns Hopkins University, 1996*

Each of you is now inheriting the dreams of your parents and the wealth of our society. It falls on your shoulders to continue our progress and protect our legacy.

*Gen. Henry H. Shelton*
*North Carolina State University, 1998*

Be bold, be bold, be bold. Keep on reading. Make time to listen to music, or look at a painting, or go to the movies, or do whatever feeds your mind....

*Susan Sontag*
*writer*
*Wellesley College, 1983*

Integrate what you believe into every single area of your life. Take your heart to work, and ask the most and best of everybody else too.

*Meryl Streep*
*Vassar College, 1983*

Don't be stopped by barriers or fears that your path will be difficult. If you want it badly enough and keep working, you can accomplish what you want.

*Chick Corea*
*Berklee, 1997*

Listen to that small voice from inside you, that tells you to go another way. George Eliot wrote, "It is never too late to be what you might have been." It is never too early, either.

*Anna Quindlen*
*Mount Holyoke College, 1999*

Though it's crucial to make a living, that shouldn't be your inspiration or your aspiration. Do it for yourself, your highest self, for your own pride, joy, ego, gratification, expression, love, fulfillment, happiness. Do it because it's what you have to do.

*Billy Joel*
*Berklee, 1993*

You'll soon discover that opportunities don't just keep showing up in your mailbox week after week like the Publishers Clearing House Sweepstakes. Rather your success will be determined by your ability to make your own opportunities. The better you get at turning defeats into victories, frustration into satisfaction, and visions into reality, the more successful you will become.

*Gen. Henry H. Shelton*
*North Carolina State University, 1998*

Be brave enough to live life creatively.

*Alan Alda*
*Connecticut College, 1980*

In your journey toward the realization of
personal goals, don't make choices based only
on your security and your safety. Nothing is
safe. It is not safe to challenge the status quo.
But challenge it you must.

*Toni Morrison*
*Barnard College, 1979*

Wherever you are, make your work matter.

*Sue Suter*
*Robert Morris College, 1996*

Don't lose touch with your capacity to see absurdity, to laugh — including at yourselves — to enjoy, to take time out from striving, and just be. Let yourself need people, and let them need you.

*Elizabeth Drew*
*journalist*
*Reed College, 1979*

If we have no sense of history, how can we recognize the challenge of now unless we remember the errors of then?

*Studs Terkel*
*journalist*
*Grinnell College, 1977*

Give up the nonsensical and punishing quest for perfection that dogs too many of us through too much of our lives.

*Anna Quindlen*
*Mount Holyoke College, 1999*

# Floss.

*Mary Schmich*
Chicago Tribune, 1997

As your emissary from the real world,
I'll share a secret. Out here we function in the
midst of doubt, we go through life adjusting and
readjusting the course, questioning its value
and our value. We are, as it says in the opening
line of the traditional will, "Mindful of the
uncertainties of life."

*Ellen Goodman*
*journalist*
*Simmons College, 1986*

Do not desire to fit in.
Desire to lead.

*Gwendolyn Brooks*
*poet*
*University of Vermont, 1986*

Throw yourself out into the convulsions of the world, live in it, look at it, witness it. Take chances, make your own work, and take pride in it.

*Joan Didion*
*writer*
*Bard College, 1987*

You are educated. Your certification is in your degree. You may think of it as the ticket to the good life. Let me ask you to think of an alternative. Think of it as your ticket to change the world.

*Tom Brokaw*
*broadcaster*
*Duke University, 1989*

Our number one problem is that not enough of us really believes that significant change is possible.

*Wendy Kopp*
*founder/president, Teach for America*
*Syracuse University, 1992*

It is your task to prove conventional wisdom
wrong and make your unpredictable dreams
come true.

*Freeman Dyson*
*scientist/writer*
*Haverford College, 1991*


Don't live down to expectations. Go out there
and do something remarkable.

*Wendy Wasserstein*
*playwright*
*Mount Holyoke College, 1990*

You cannot help but learn more as you take the world into your hands. Take it up reverently, for it is an old piece of clay, with millions of thumbprints on it.

*John Updike*
*author*
*University of Massachusetts at Amherst, 1993*

Eleanor Roosevelt said once that "within all of us there are two sides. One reaches for the stars, the other descends to the level of beasts. That is not only a statement of fact. It is a presentation of choice.

*Madeleine Albright*
*former U.S. Secretary of State*
*Barnard College, 1995*

W e all have this inner strength within us. Just rely on that solid foundation that you have started building with the education you've received.

*Christopher Reeve*
*actor*
*Williams College, 1999*

# Chapter 7

# This Land
# Is Your Land

Freedom's natural derivatives are people doing what they want to do and benefiting from their own effort.

*Orrin Hatch*
*Dixie College*

Cherish your freedom of choice.

*Chick Corea*
*Berklee, 1997*

Every man sent out from a university should
be a man of his nation as well as a man of
his time.

*Woodrow Wilson*
*28th president of the United States*
*from the JFK speech at Yale, 1963*

Give something to the community in one way
or another. It doesn't have to be dramatic, it
doesn't have to be in the newspapers. But you
need to have the satisfaction of knowing you're
helping make somebody else's life a little
brighter.

*George Bush*
*Johns Hopkins University, 1996*

No matter what you do or how busy you are, there is always a way to serve a larger community. It doesn't matter what laws we pass or what programs we put in place. We cannot reverse decades of patterns of behavior unless more of our citizens are willing to take some responsibility for helping those who need help.

*Bill Clinton*
*42nd president of the United States*
*Penn State, 1996*

The community instructs the young in the ways of the past. And we should honor those before us as we hope to be honored by those to whom we pass along our treasures, our knowledge and our skills.

*Robert Pinsky*
*U.S. poet laureate*
*Stanford, 1999*

If you can accept the fact that your solutions too will be incomplete, and yet not let that possibility, that fear paralyze you into inaction and indifference, you may still be able to achieve a safer and a better, if a still imperfect, world.

*Edward W. Brooke*
*U.S. Senator, Massachusetts*
*Syracuse University*

I speak of peace as the necessary rational end of rational men.

*John F. Kennedy*
*Yale, 1963*

I suggest to you that a free press is an irreplaceable source of power to a free people. Further, I suggest to you that it is a fragile right that must be guarded zealously.

*Tom Brokaw*
*Syracuse University, 1979*

There are two forms of disaster which can overtake a nation. One is silence — when the voices of all the observers and commentators, the analysts and critics have been stilled. The other is chaos — when everyone is babbling at the same time.

*Ted Koppel*
*Tufts University, 1994*

America is a promise and a hope in the minds and hearts of all those who cherish liberty, justice, and opportunity.

*Hubert Humphrey*
*former U.S. vice president*
*University of Pennsylvania, 1977*

We must become aware of our own unique role in this world and our own unique responsibility. We must develop an awareness which enables us to evaluate any deeds, actions, or purposes from the viewpoint of their global consequences.

*Mikhail Gorbachev*
*Emory University, 1992*

In the dialogues of Plato, a main thesis was that a human being's greatest goal is happiness. The state of happiness can be attained by leading a morally and ethically good life. Develop a set of habits which make you choose right instead of wrong almost automatically. That is what makes you a good person, which is even more important than being a successful one.

*Ahmet Ertegun*
*Berklee, 1991*

# Chapter 8

# Do the Right Thing

I am convinced that when we do the things that make us the happiest, the universe responds.

*Renee Magriel Roberts, Ph.D.*
*commencement response*
*Union Institute, 1998*


I do not deny that many appear to have succeeded in a material way by cutting corners and manipulating associates.But material success is possible in this world and far more satisfying when it comes without exploiting others.

*Alan Greenspan*
*Federal Reserve chairman*
*Harvard, 1999*


I believe that any definition of a successful life must include service to others.

*George Bush*
*The Johns Hopkins University, 1996*

There is honor in doing your best.

*Orrin Hatch*
*Dixie College*

Indelibly impressed upon me when I was a child, an adolescent, and even today, was to tell the truth. When people are dishonest, families are broken, individuals are ruined, governments are toppled. As Hobbes said, "Hell is realizing the truth too late."

*Dan Quayle*
*former U.S. Senator and vice president*
*DePauw University*

Live your life from truth and you will survive everything.

*Oprah Winfrey*
*Wellesley College, 1997*

I am only one,
But still I am one,
I cannot do everything,
But still I can do something,
And because I cannot do everything,
I will not refuse to do the something
that I can do.

*Edward Everett Hale*
*from a speech by Vernon Jordan,*
*University of Pennsylvania, 1981*

The true measure of a career is to be able to be content, even proud, that you succeeded through your own endeavors.

*Alan Greenspan*
*Harvard, 1999*

The rule of law and majority rule will not work unless we establish stronger foundations of mutual understanding and tolerance. That requires that we speak out positively, candidly and constructively, with purpose, with collegiality, with thoughtfulness.

*Janet Reno*
*Northwestern Law School, 2000*

If you stick to your integrity and your goals, eventually the world will appreciate what you are doing.

*Bonnie Raitt*
*Berklee, 1992*

$M$ay each of us be blessed with
confidence and the fibre of moral
certainty as we are confronted by our
daily trials and tests.

*Ted Koppel*
*Tufts University, 1994*

We all pay for our choices, and whatever life we choose determines the kind of rewards we earn. There is a palpable moral component to our beings, and it can be contaminated. Moral contamination almost never announces itself, it is always a very small, seemingly silent, inconsequential event, but it is like radiation, it accumulates, and there are no permissible safe levels.

*E.L. Doctorow*
*Hobart and William Smith Colleges, 1979*

A generation from now, as you watch your children graduate, you will want to be able to say that whatever success you achieved was the result of honest and productive work and that you dealt with people the way you would want them to deal with you.

*Alan Greenspan*
*Harvard, 1999*

Regardless of the next steps for you, regardless of what career you devote your life to in the coming period, please give a little of yourself to others.

*Johnnetta Cole*
*Williams College, 1989*

Please do this world and your honorable profession one small favor. Give back. Remember the people struggling alongside you and below you: the people who haven't had the same opportunity, the same blessings, the same education, the same degree.

*Tim Russert*
*broadcaster*
*Catholic University, The Columbus School of Law, 1997*

What makes being alive worthwhile to me is the saints I meet. They could be almost anywhere. By saints I mean people who behave decently and honorably.

*Kurt Vonnegut*
*author*
*Syracuse University, 1994*

Everything you do is a self-portrait. The way you treat people above you, and below you, paints a picture of what kind of person you are.

*Wendy Walker Whitworth*
*TV producer*
*Hollins College, 1996*

Though the suffering may indeed be great, it is nothing compared to the joy of doing the right thing.

*Mumia Abu-Jamal*
*activist/writer*
*Evergreen State College, 1999*

$B$e as bold as the first man
to eat an oyster.

*Shirley Chisholm*
*U.S. congresswoman*
*Mount Holyoke College, 1981*

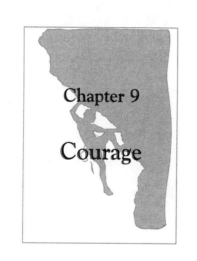

Chapter 9

Courage

Right now you are new graduates with minds open to many ideas and points of view.... Keep those minds open.

*Jane Bryant Quinn*
*Middlebury College, 1981*

You cannot be consistently kind, or true, or fair, or generous, or honest, without courage. I wish I had said that first; actually, Aristotle said it.

*Maya Angelou*
*writer/poet*
*Simmons College, 1987*

Y ou are the generation God has chosen to save this planet ....As Martin Luther King, Jr. said, "Every crisis has both its dangers and its opportunities." Our hope is that you who are graduating will seize the opportunity to make us a new world, where peace, prosperity, and justice are secured for all people.

*Coretta Scott King*
*activist and writer*
*Denison University, 1983*

A life lived deliberately has been the example of people I admire and respect.

*Mumia Abu-Jamal*
*Evergreen State College, 1999*

There is an incredible resilience in a people....There is something in the human spirit that refuses to be quenched.

*Desmond Tutu*
*1984 Nobel Peace Prize recipient*
*Wesleyan University, 1990*

While you're setting goals, don't be afraid of failure. Fear of failure is a far worse condition than failure itself, because it kills off possibilities. The worst thing that can happen if you risk failure is that you will fail.

*Michael Eisner*
*CEO, Disney*
*Denison University, 1989*

What's interesting about failure is how you handle it.

*Bob Edwards*
*radio broadcaster*
*Grinnell College, 1991*

Success is never final; failure is never fatal;
the only thing that matters is courage.

*Winston Churchill*
*from Sandra Day O'Connor's speech*
*Rockford College, 1989*

Courage is the most important of all the virtues because without courage you cannot be sure that you can practice any other virtue with consistency.

*Maya Angelou*
*Smith College, 1980*

Abraham Lincoln did not go to Gettysburg having commissioned a poll to find out what would sell at Gettysburg. There were no people with percentages for him, cautioning him about this group or that group or what they found in exit polls a year earlier. We need the courage of Lincoln.

*Robert Coles*
*psychiatrist/writer*
*Beloit College, 1984*

There was a wonderful lady who once said to me, "It ain't how good you are, Pearl. It's how long you can last." I have got a friend now who is sick with double cancer. Double. On both sides. And I told her this story one day, and she laughed, this courageous woman. She said, "So right, Pearl. But may I add something? You got to be good to last." That is the answer.

*Pearl Bailey*
*entertainer*
*Syracuse University, 1985*

Identity is something that one must create for himself by choices that are significant and that require a courageous commitment in the face of anguish and risk. Identity is one's witness to truth in one's life.

*Thomas Merton*
*from Julius Lester's speech*
*Hampshire College, 1984*

We all need to practice and improve. But I did think when I was younger that there would be a day when I would sort of "get it", and that everything would be perfect, and I would have arrived at that promised land. And I can see now that that perfection is never going to happen.

*Pat Matheney*
*Berklee, 1996*

# Chapter 10

# The Future Is Now

You're not freshmen now, and there isn't going to be another freshman year for you as there was when you graduated high school. This is different. The apron strings are finally cut; and you're graduating as whole people.

*Madeleine L'Engle*
*Smith College, 1977*

The test for this century is whether we mistake a growth of wealth and power for a growth in strength and character.

*Vince Lombardi*
*from a speech by Sam Nunn*
*Emory University, 1981*

However nostalgic we are about the children that you once were, we love and admire the adults you have become.

*Stephen Breyer*
*Stanford, 1997*

If you can bring to your children the self that you truly are, as opposed to some amalgam of manners and mannerisms, expectations and fears that you have acquired as a carapace along the way, you will give them, too, a great gift.

*Anna Quindlen*
*Mount Holyoke College 1999*

Let me remind you that every day, today, and every tomorrow, is an end in itself. The trick of getting to a cherished goal on some final day … is to live fully each day to the full as an end in itself.

*Robert Thurman*
*professor/writer*
*Hampshire College, 1983*

Not everyone can be a philosopher. But every thinking person should reflect on the future, and meditate about the destiny of mankind here on earth.

*Mikhail Gorbachov*
*Emory University, 1992*

I am not worried about your economic future....this is a prosperous land. I am worried about your moral vision and purpose.... We are the luckiest people that ever lived, we have abundantly and manifestly the capacity to address human problems if we care. It is a matter of vision and courage and compassion.

*Ramsey Clark*
*former U.S. Attorney General*
*University of Santa Clara, 1978*

For the young person who who insists there is more to life than this, who believes with the prairie poet that "youth when lighted and alive and given a sporting chance is strong for struggle," there are new adventures and new knowledge.

*Studs Terkel*
*Grinnell College, 1977*

You're heading out on an adventure, and you can always change your mind along the way and try something else. I know lots of people who have done that, and none I can think of who regret it.

*Tracy Kidder*
*Sarah Lawrence College, 1986*

You'll remember the king in *Alice in Wonderland*. When asked, "Where shall I begin?" the king says, "Begin at the beginning, and go on until you come to the end; then stop." What I am suggesting is that you stop at the beginning, stop at your commencement. It's not very interesting to stop at the end — I mean everyone does that. So stop now. Tell them you won't go. Go back to your rooms. Unpack!

*George Plimpton*
*Harvard University, 1977*

In an effort to find a phrase or a word that I would like to pass on as inspirational, I thought about what best expressed the theme of my own life. Passion! It's the force that has governed and motivated all my energies, that has given me the discipline that is mandatory to all creative efforts, and without it, life seems to me rather bleak and dismal.

*Neil Simon*
*Williams College, 1984*

Go to work for the person you admire the most. Something good will come of it. Emulate your hero as best you can.

*Warren Buffett*
*businessman/entrepreneur,*
*from the speech by Thomas Winship*
*Marlboro College, 1985*

I think our future lies behind us. In the last dozen years, I have learned many things, but that history is our greatest teacher is perhaps the most important lesson.

*Ken Burns*
*documentarian*
*Hampshire College, 1987*

Ultimately, it is you — alone with your conscience, your intelligence, your life's experience — who determine what you believe you owe to others. How you think about the needs of strangers will determine the kind of society we become.

*Bill Bradley*
*U.S. Senator, New Jersey*
*Dartmouth College, 1987*

In the time you have left, make the most of it by making the most of yourself, which is doing what means the most to you and not to somebody else.

*Malcolm Forbes*
*Syracuse University, 1988*

Schooling, for many of you, is over, but your education is still continuing.

*Steve Kroft*
*Syracuse University, 1996*

Endings need not be public, newsworthy events. Throughout your life, there will be many little endings, every day. It is these endings that somehow give shape to the fragments of your life that are called experience. And it is this "experience" that makes up one's life.

*James V. Cunningham*
*poet*
*Lawrence University, 1978*

Casey Stengel said, "I never make predictions — at least not about the future." And I can see why. Consider…1895: The president of the British Royal Society predicts, "Heavier-than-air flying machines are impossible." 1899: The chief of the U.S. Patent Office announces: "Everything that can be invented has been invented." 1927: The head of Warner Brothers asks, "Who wants to hear actors talk?" 1943: Tom Watson, the president of IBM, announces, "I think there is a world market for maybe five computers." 1949: *Popular Mechanics* points out, "Computers in the future may weigh no more than 1.5 tons." Neither I nor you can be certain how your lives will unfold; we cannot predict.

*Stephen Breyer*
*Colby College, 1998*

Life is not about writing great books, amassing great wealth or achieving great power. It is about loving and being loved. It is about savoring the beauty of moments that don't last.

*Rabbi Harold Kushner*
*from a speech by Sue Suter*
*Robert Morris College, 1996*

# Chapter 11

# The Last Word

$A$t the end of your life, you will never regret
not having passed one more test, not winning
one more verdict or not closing one more deal.
You will regret time not spent with a husband,
a child, a friend or a parent.

*Barbara Bush*
*Wellesley College*

$T$wo roads diverged in a wood, and I—
I took the one less traveled by,
And that has made all the difference.

*Robert Frost*
*from John Fitzgerald Kennedy's speech*
*Amherst College, 1963*

$W$e need to find a cause that summons us to
unselfishness. Personal integrity, our moral
compass, counts far more than any line on a
resume.

*Elizabeth Dole*
*Johns Hopkins University, 1998*

Sometimes we just need to set up the right circumstances and allow people to follow their own stars.

*Raymond W. Smith*
*Carnegie Mellon University, 1997*

Let us not be blind to our differences—but let us also direct attention to our common interests and to the means by which those differences can be resolved. And if we cannot end now our differences, at least we can help make the world safe for diversity. For, in the final analysis, our most basic common link is that we all inhabit this small planet. We all breathe the same air. We all cherish our children's future. And we are all mortal.

*John F. Kennedy*
*Yale, 1963*

Be bold in your dreaming, be bold in your living, be bold in your caring, your compassion, your humanity and then, when you sit at your grandchild's commencement half a century from now, you'll look back at the tapestry of your life and find it good, and that will be the greatest success of all.

*George Bush*
*The Johns Hopkins University, 1996*

It's the process of trying that's significant. That's where all the messy, beautiful human stuff lies — in the space between the "you" and the "other," between the "you" and the "I."

*Jodie Foster*
*actress*
*Yale University, 1992*

By law no commencement speech can end without a list of Benjamin Franklin-like practical suggestions. So here they are.

- Call your mother frequently.
- In your own role as mothers or fathers, spend more time with your children than you think reasonable.
- Pay attention to your habits, because pretty soon they become your life.
- Always write angry letters to your enemies. Never mail them. This way you get the anger out of your system while minimizing the amount of your time that is controlled by those you dislike.
- Disbelieve both the best and the worst that others say about you. Realize that whatever you say about people will inevitably get back to them.

*James Fallows*
*Medill School of Journalism*
*Northwestern University, 1996*

Pessimists calculate the odds. Optimists believe they can overcome them.

*Ted Koppel*
*Tufts University, 1994*

Enjoy your body....Don't be afraid of it or of what other people think of it.

*Mary Schmich*
*Chicago Tribune, 1997*

Lord knows that it is hard to get to the top, but it is a darned sight harder staying there.

*George Martin*
*Berklee, 1989*

Sometimes you're ahead, sometimes you're behind. The race is long and, in the end, it's only with yourself.

*Mary Schmich*
Chicago Tribune, 1997

The true bottom line is, and will always be, talent and excellence. Whatever you decide to do, the important thing is to do it well. You can't always find the job or opportunity you may most desire, but whatever job you do get, do it well. And it will lead to other opportunities.

*Ahmet Ertegun*
*Berklee, 1991*

The heart does not know how to think in terms of self-fulfillment; the heart is made for love.

*Madeleine L'Engle*
*Smith College, 1977*

Understand that friends come and go, but with a precious few you should hold on. The older you get, the more you need the people who knew you when you were young.

*Mary Schmich*
Chicago Tribune, 1997

The best things said come last. People will talk for hours saying nothing much and then linger at the door with words that come with a rush from the heart.

*Alan Alda*
*Connecticut College, 1980*

You can sleep in your old age if you live long enough to enjoy it.

*Beverly Sills*
*opera singer*
*Smith College, 1985*

There is nothing wrong with idealism, no matter what the cynics say.

*Thomas Winship*
*Marlboro College, 1985*

We aren't leaving you a blueprint to solve your problems, but then nobody gave us one either. We were on our own. And guess what? So are you.

*Lee Iacocca*
*Duke University, 1986*

What Moses brought down from Mount Sinai were not the Ten Suggestions; they are commandments. Are, not were. The sheer beauty of the commandments is that they codify, in a handful of words, acceptable human behavior, not just for then or now, but for all time. Language evolves, power shifts from nation to nation, messages are transmitted with the speed of light, man erases one frontier after another; and yet we, and our behavior, and the commandments which govern that behavior, remain the same.

*Ted Koppel*
*Duke University, 1987*

Since life is our most precious gift, and since it is given to us to live but once, let us live so we will not regret years of inertia, and timidity.

*Maya Angelou*
*Simmons College, 1987*

Happy endings are the rule rather than the exception out of the experiences of my own life and the observation of my eyes and mind. The way of the world is no river of experience, but it is no mean blind alley of hopelessness, either. It's just this street that goes someplace.

*Stephen King*
*University of Maine, 1988*

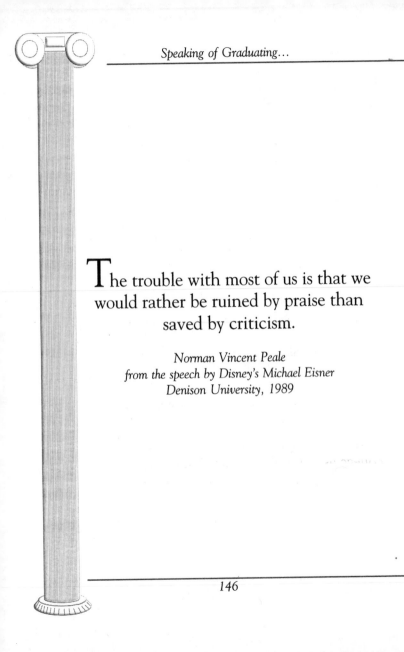

The trouble with most of us is that we would rather be ruined by praise than saved by criticism.

*Norman Vincent Peale*
*from the speech by Disney's Michael Eisner*
*Denison University, 1989*

Not to know is bad. Not to want to know is worse. Not to hope is unthinkable. Not to care unforgivable.

> *Igbo people of Nigeria*
> *from Johnnetta Cole's address*
> *Williams College, 1989*

Never think that life is not worth living, or that you can't make a difference.

> *Marian Wright Edelman*
> *University of Illinois at Champaign-Urbana, 1993*

This afternoon, I solemnly promise you that these have not been the best years of your life. The truth is that people who look back to college as the peak experience have had the dreariest of adulthoods. I don't wish that on any of you.

> *Ellen Goodman*
> *Smith College, 1993*

Success is a spiral with trying, failing, learning, and growing, and that's what excellence is.

*Ben Cohen*
*co-founder, Ben and Jerry's*
*Hampshire College, 1990*

Excellence is an internal quality, a consequence in large measure of the capacity and of the commitment of an individual. Excellence endures.

*Thomas Boswell*
*from the address by Hearst president Cathleen Black*
*Simmons College, 1990*

Excellence is doing your best
at what you do best.

*Cathleen Black*
*Simmons College, 1990*

Carry laughter with you wherever you go.

*Hugh Sidey*
*Coe College, 1995*

I wish you the ability to trust your instincts, follow your passions, and to find the ability to pursue a life where love of work and love of self are combined.

*Annette Bening*
*actress*
*San Francisco State University, 1995*

Ronald Reagan has a sign on his desk that I put on mine. It says, "There is no limit what you can do or where you can go as long as you don't mind who gets the credit."

*Wendy Walker Whitworth*
*Hollins College, 1996*

In all things in life, choose your conscience, and trust your instincts, and lead your lives without regrets.

*David Halberstam*
*author*
*Dartmouth College, 1996*

The first rule is this: Cherish your friends and your family as if your life depended on it...because it does.

*Ann Richards*
*Mount Holyoke College, 1995*

I beg you, cherish the day,
live it, enjoy it, savor it.

*Mary Higgins Clark*
*author*
*Providence College, 1996*

$M$ost of all, dare to reach out your hand into the darkness, to pull another hand into the light.

*Norman B. Rice*
*professor*
*Whitman College, 1998*

$S$ee, feel, question, explore, experience, walk, dance, run, play, eat, love, learn, dare, taste, touch, smell, listen, argue, speak, write, read, draw, provoke, emote, scream, cry, kneel, pray, pray often, bow, rise, stand, look, sing, embrace the questions, be wary of answers, create, cajole, confront, confound, walk backward, walk forward, circle, hide, seek, say no, say yes, embrace, follow your heart, trust your heart, engage love again and again on this beautiful, broken world.

*Terry Tempest Williams*
*writer*
*College of the Atlantic, 1999*

When people are laughing, they're generally
not killing each other.

*Alan Alda*
*Connecticut College, 1980*

Cherish your human connections:
your relationships with family and friends are
among the most important investments you
will ever make.

*Barbara Bush*
*Wellesley College, 1989*

# Ladies and gentlemen of the class of '97: Wear sunscreen.

*Mary Schmich*
Chicago Tribune

# And in conclusion: Go get 'em.

*Paul Newman*
*Sarah Lawrence College, 1989*

# Index

*About the Author*

Alan Ross is a writer and sports historian living with his wife, Karol Cooper, in Monteagle, Tennessee. A graduate of Fordham University, he is a former editor for Professional Team Publications, Athlon Sports Communications, and Walnut Grove Press. His feature articles on sports history have appeared in *The Sporting News*, *Lindy's Pro Football*, *Athlon Sports Pro Football*, *Athletic Administration*, *Game Day*, *NFL Insider*, *Arizona Cardinals Media Guide*, *The Coffin Corner* and *Track Record*. Ross is also the history columnist for *Titans Exclusive*, the official fan publication of the NFL's Tennessee Titans. He has authored six sports books. This is his fourth non-sports book for WALNUT GROVE PRESS.

For more information
about WALNUT GROVE PRESS books
call 1-800-256-8584